21 GEMS

Lyncia Creado

BookLeaf Publishing

LYNCIA CREADO

21 Gems © 2023 Lyncia Creado

All rights reserved.

Presentation by *BookLeaf Publishing*

Web: www.bookleafpub.com E-mail: info@bookleafpub.com

ISBN: 9789357697866

First edition 2023

I dedicate this book

To my beloved mother Dr. Nymphia Correa,
who passed away on 24th May, 2021;

To my husband Astor, my children Shane, Thea
& Vanya, my father (late) Hyginus and all those
who have made a positive difference in my life;

To every person who dares to dream, and
who believes in themselves;

And of course, to the Almighty, whom I thank
for what He has done for me and without whom
this book of poems wouldn't be possible.

ACKNOWLEDGEMENT

I wish to express my gratitude to BookLeaf
Publishing for appreciating my poetry
compositions and publishing them.
A special thank you to my daughter Thea for
encouraging me to *rite and publish my poems.

PREFACE

It is said that poetry is the language of the soul. '21 Gems' is my soul journey through life, through its ebbs and flows.

I have divided this journey into four phases: The Wonder Years, Adulthood, Sunset Years and the Afterlife. Every poem I have composed is a spontaneous overflow of powerful feelings

related to my state of mind during incidents that have crossed my path, coloured with emotion. I hope the simple language I have used

resonates with every reader, and that every one of you reading this can find something you identify with.

THE WONDER YEARS

ALL I HAD AND DID

It doesn't seem too long ago
When I was just a kid,
I clearly can recall it all,
The things I had and did!

Sugar-coated gummy bears,
Coffee chocolate, bubble gum,
Cotton candy, ice-cream pops,
And Christmas cake with rum.

Spinning tops, marbles, flying kites,
Hopscotch and Chor police,
Were fun games that we played each day -
But the best was hide and seek.

We dressed our dolls and played house,
While our brothers had mini cars,
Their super-heroes like He-man,
With their super hero powers!

And when we fell and hurt ourselves,
Iodine and Mercurochrome was the cure,
But nothing ever stopped us,
From the urge of playing more!

Soda-stoppers, tazos, stamps and coins,
Were all our precious treasures,
The wrist-watch that we wore with pride
Gave contentment without measure.

Influenza was a common excuse,
When we wanted to bunk school,
But with measles, mumps and chicken pox,
We couldn't play the fool!

Nancy Drew, The Brothers Grimm,
Enid Blyton in place of Rowling,
Made our fantasies run riot,
It was truly astounding!

We'd call to friends across the road,
Had a whistle signal too,
No mobile phones and apps to use,
Matchbox phones with strings would do.

We rode our bicycles and played cards,
Devised places we'd never seen,
And when it came to Cluedo,
I was always Mustard Green!

We climbed trees, scraped our knees,
Ate tamarind and raw mango,
Street food from the carts was great,
We couldn't ask for more.

Music was on the radio gram,
Then came records and cassettes,
And every household had volumes high,
To show off all their assets.

Wrangler jeans and Bata shoes
Were the latest trend,
Pleated skirts, bell bottomed pants,
Were fashions on which we'd spend.

Simple things - they mattered much,
And gave us so much pleasure,
The precious time with family,
Was valued much and treasured.

Daily rosary at the cross,
And grace before our meals,
Sunday mass was regular,
With dresses, hats and heels

And while I reminisce today
On those happy care-free days,
I am grateful for all I had and did,
In so many different ways.

TEENAGE YEARS

At thirteen I realized I was no longer a child
Not an adult, uncertain and wild.

My parents I thought, were old fashioned and weird
At their dress sense and ideas - I jestingly sneered.

With my friends I would go out to clubs every night,
Fast food and pastries - A great appetite.

The clothes that I wore were of the latest trend,
Keeping up with the joneses and all my good friends.

Rock music I loved, and it was played loud -
On my Sharp amplifier, of which I was proud.

I craved independence and wished to explore,
A world that was filled with opportunities galore.

I wanted to build a life for myself
By learning to step out - Not staying on the shelf.

A rebel I was, so stubborn and bold
Misunderstood by many, and out of control.

Yet as I grew up and reached adulthood
I slowly grew sober and learned what I could.

And today as I look back, On those restless years;
I'm thankful they happened - Those mad teenage years!

LIFE IS LIKE A GAME OF CARDS

Life is like a game of cards -
We shuffle, cut and deal;
You can't choose what you get in hand -
Round goes the fortune wheel.

We play the game and follow rules -
We can't go out of turn;
And when it comes to gambling -
Take chances, lose or earn.

Some of us are dealt high cards,
And others very low;
Some may have no trumps to call,
They move on with the flow.

The suits within the deck of cards,
They represent life's journey;
If hearts are up, you're in for love,
The skies are bright and sunny!

When clubs are but the ruling suit,
Take care look out for war;
Greed and envy is the root,
Beware of what you draw

Diamonds are a girl's best friend,
They tell of wealth and money;
Take heed of women who befriend,
A man for milk and honey

And when a darkened spade is in,
It speaks of manual labour;
Of toiling slaves who lost their lives,
For masters cruel to favour.

Yes, life is like a game of cards,
We play with our free will;
But always being on our guard,
With strategy and skill.

YOU ARE ENOUGH

Believe in yourself, and always remember
You don't have to change to please the other gender.

Model the respect you seek in a partner,
Only fight fairly and don't be a martyr.

Care for your body and you'll be drawn very soon,
To someone who's swell, on you he will swoon.

Don't get lost in a relationship - keep hobbies, friends and time,
If not, it is meaningless, and not worth a dime.

A man who ridicules his mum or his sis
Could behave the same with you once you're his.

So keep a keen eye, and listen with care
To red flags that show up You must be aware.

Reenacting the past, outside pressure, shared friends
Aren't good enough reasons for relationships to mend.

Know what you want, have a strong sense of self;
Don't try to be what another man yens.

Life isn't easy, nor is it fair;
But choices are yours - Don't give up on prayer.

ADULTHOOD

THE ART OF LIVING

Living in the now and worrying what may be
Could ruin a perfect present.
Remember your past made you what you are,
Keep away from what you shouldn't.

Be thankful for each new day that may come
Be daring and willing to try,
A brave heart will win and never succumb
But only if you set your aim high.

You need to get out of your comfort zone
Each morning do something you dare
Don't be hooked to your mobile phone
Time won't wait if you stand and you stare.

Trust your instincts, don't let yourself down,
Your best friend is in the mirror.
Keep your family and your good friends around,
Move forward with zest and with rigour.

Opportunity knocks only once at your door
So step while the tide is in,
When you reach your target, don't crave more,
Happiness comes from within.

FENCES

We build all types of fences,
In our own subconscious mind.
Fences sturdy, fences strong,
They leave woe and strife behind

These fences hold back arguments,
Silence the evil tongue,
They help to keep the trouble out,
When all is said and done.

Yet there are other fences built,
By those who hold a grudge.
They keep rejected people out.
But who are we to judge?

There are fences between man and wife,
Some among siblings too,
These wretched little fences,
Make animosity spew.

Fences built by the youth today,
They keep the parents out.
The 'generation gap' it's called,
That creates war and doubt

Fences fail to let us grow,
Like they do with flowers and fruit.
We need to sort our problems,
And tackle them from the root

So try and keep an open mind,
And take a different view;
Allow for love and laughter,
And don't make much ado.

The fence that keeps the problems out,
Could also keep them in,
So move ahead and break that fence,
You'll soon succeed and win.

THE CHOICE IS YOURS

There are times in life you need to choose,
Between the good and ugly.
And oft you tend to step aside,
Sit on the shelf so snugly.

Be it a partner or job to choose,
You simply just can't figure -
For fear of choosing wrongly,
And the problem then grows bigger.

You dilly-dally on the way,
Precious time put to the test;
When questioned, you must have your say,
You think you know it best.

Although you have the actual facts,
You pretend to have no clue;
It's the ego that has great impact,
And puts you in a stew.

So to hide away what's in your mind,
You dive into the dark;
In your comfort zone you play it blind,
On shaky ground embark.

And lo! the choice you've make is bad,
But who are they to judge?
It's yours to handle, yours to deal,
They have no right to grudge

Then, to cover up your grave mistake,
You point a finger at others;
While quietly wallowing in misery,
Depression sets in and smothers.

So when at times you need to choose,
Between bad good or the best,
Don't take a risk, think loud, be wise,
Make sure you pass the test.

WHAT IS LOVE?

Love is patient,
Love is kind,
Love is not jealous,
So hard to find!

Love does not envy,
Love is not proud,
Love does not boast,
Love is not loud.

Love is not angered,
It keeps no record,
It always protects,
Doesn't act by the sword.

It delights not in evil,
But rejoices with truth,
Has no room for doubt,
And misused by the youth.

Love is not hesitant,
It keeps you at ease,
It's calm and collected,
You feel so at peace.

Love is not anxious,
It's not touch and go,
Love is not troubled,
With time it just grows.

You don't walk on thin ice,
When you truly love,
It's a gift from the universe,
A sheer velvet glove.

LIFE IS A GIFT

I kept to myself,
they said I was snobbish.
I talked about life,
they thought I was foolish.

They wanted direction,
then questioned my lead,
Went their own way,
paid no attention or heed.

I spoke of achievement,
they thought I was mad,
I told them my dreams,
they said those were sad.

They pretended to listen,
but paid a deaf ear,
Then tried to console me,
said I had nothing to fear.

I spent all that time with them
doing what I could,
To change their impression
and trying to do good.

Alas! all my actions
were but spent in vain,
They wanted a woman
they could bind down with chains.

Then I questioned myself,
what was best for my being?
Instead of compliance
and easily agreeing.

So for solace I walked
to the seaside and gazed,
At each wave that broke
on the shore so unphased.

I buckled up courage,
believed in myself;
Faced the imposters,
was ready for hell.

From mother nature I learned,
that life is a gift.
Time is not guaranteed,
it races by so swift.

So live life the manner
you would like it to be,
Don't worry about others,
just breathe and be free.

LOVE YOUR FAMILY

The choicest garb, the sweetest grace
Are oft to strangers shown
The careless mien, the frowning face
Are given to our own.

We flatter those we scarcely know,
We please the fleeting guest.
And deal many a thoughtless blow
To those who love us best.

How often do we set aside,
A few moments to make a call?
To our very own family members whom
We rarely see at all?

Are we concerned, about how much time,
Has passed since we last met?
And are we sure, we can afford,
To sit back and forget?

Does the strange friend, seem a true friend
When you travel far away?
Don't waste your life, to strive for joy,
It was always there to stay.

For it's the old home roof, that shelters,
All the charm that life can give;
There you find the safest place,
The happiest spot to live

Your family is like a circle,
The connection never ends
And even if at times it breaks,
In time it always mends.

Family defines, just who you are
And will be a part of you,
No matter if you stray afar
The traits will stick like glue.

THE TEST

You put me through the test each time ,
Through fire, rain and pain;
And that's the time I ask you Lord,
Is my life all in vain?

Ever since I was a child,
You taught me not to fail,
And brought me out of troubled times,
Whether night or day.

In hospital I laid in bed,
So many times before;
Not knowing if I'd see day light,
When almost at death's door.

I went to prison for a term,
That I was not to serve,
Was someone else who performed the crime,
A man who had no nerve.

Last night you tested me again,
While dinner was being laid,
And in the kitchen, I bent down,
To light the oven flame

Suddenly - there was a blast,
And the fire raged at me,
My hair got singed, my dress was scorched
But You came in between

I thank you Lord for all the tests,
That you have given me,
Although at times it seems unfair,
I know you're here with me.

I ask you Lord to give me strength,
To pass each test with ease,
For life is hard and full of hurt,
And not just hurdle free.

SUNSET YEARS

SKIES ARE GETTING DARK

As years roll by, you'll find in time,
Your skies are getting dark.
Your seventies, eighties, nineties,
Are where you have now embarked.

Your parents - they might not be there,
Your siblings could be farther,
Your friends are few, your children too,
Have left for greener pastures.

Weak bones and muscles, aches and pains,
Are guests who come to stay,
And literally your mind gets hazy,
You can't push them away.

Your bed is your companion,
Just like when you were born,
But no mothers love except a nurse,
Who looks at you with scorn.

So let us make the most of life,
Not keep things for the after,
Time doesn't pause – in fact we find,
It seems to pass much faster.

Hardly the day has just begun,
When we see the sun is setting.
It's barely Monday morning
And the weekend is resetting.

Say everything you need to say,
Do all that you can do,
The after may not always come,
We cannot pick and choose.

Enjoy each fleeting moment
Make sure to leave your mark,
Then sit back and smile at the happy times,
When your skies are getting dark.

JUST 7 DAYS

(DEDICATED TO MY MOTHER)

A week before she slipped and fell,
A rib she broke, but none could tell.

She bore the pain, she didn't complain,
But through her smile, we saw her change.

From then she lost her taste for food,
For brandy, honey, not in the mood.

Awake at night but slept by day,
She knew her time was ebbing away.

Her wardrobes she did clean and clear,
Phoned all the folk whom she held dear,

Requested her grandchild to compile her book,
Of life stories and the effort she took.

The lockdown took a toll on her,
No shopping sprees, no joy no cheer;

In no time, she grew weak and thin,
Just seven days had done her in.

Then Sunday came all full of hope,
She called her daughters and she spoke;

And just within an hour or so,
We heard that she had taken low

To the hospital she had to go,
Her tests were clear, but oxygen low

They made her wait in the emergency ward,
No water, food or IV cord;

For 6 hours she lay on a stretcher bed,
Until her room in the ward prepared.

The hospital staff didn't care at all,
Just another patient after all.

They started her on iv drip,
But slowly she was losing grip.

She fell into a deep, deep sleep,
Seemed at rest, her heart still beat.

The doc in charge called it a day,
We couldn't let her go away.

A cardiologist was called on sight,
But she was set for her final flight.

All too soon it was in vain,
Mummy conquered ills and pain.

With confidence she had her way,
To join my dad, we had no say.

But now she looks on us from far,
She is our helping guiding star.

An angel dressed in robe of white,
Our darling Mummy, shining bright.

A RAY OF HOPE

She lived on hope so did not fear,
When skies grew dark and grey,
A ray of hope was always there,
To wipe her tears away.

Whether it was her child return,
Or grandchild come to stay,
That ray of hope was always bright
Despair was far away.

When family members fell ill at times,
She prayed that they'd get well,
Was hope that kept the flame alive,
A hope that none could quell.

When insult and injury was thrown,
And frail her body was,
She stood the test, didn't say a word,
Hope shielded her like gauze.

Resilient, strong willed, happy with,
The little things in life,
Though the lockdown wouldn't let her out,
Her hope was still alive.

Solved crossword puzzles, wrote three books,
On real life incidents,
And hoped that times to come
would be Better or equivalent

Her food intake was almost nil,
Didn't care much for riches,
She treated every person well,
And hoped she made no glitches.

Alas that hope was fading fast,
She went into depression,
A fatal fall that did it all
To fly away, her mission.

She didn't wish to trouble fam,
She didn't speak of pain,
Phone calls to her loved ones stopped,
Seemed hope was all in vain.

Yet in her heart there still remained
A tiny ray of hope,
This time that hope was not the same,
Defiant, hard to cope.

She hoped that the Almighty,
Would take her soon someday,
Her work on Earth was all well done,
And with hope she flew away.

AFTERLIFE

HOW DO YOU SPEND YOUR TIME IN HEAVEN?

Mum, how do you spend your time in heaven?
Do you still wake at a half past seven?

And who prepares your morning tea?
Do you ever get to watch TV?

And have you time to draw and paint?
The angels there must find that quaint.

Do you and dad teach them to tango?
And do you play tunes on the piano?

They must enjoy your company
And gaze at you so wondrously.

Have you taught them of ferns and flowers?
Like you did on Earth with us for hours?

Does Dad display his puppet shows
And keep the angels on their toes?

And are you watching us from there?
Since you left, life seems so bare.

In heaven, are there Mills and Boon,
Those you read each afternoon?

I miss your smile, your warm embrace,
Your loving arms, none can replace.

Yet, I feel your presence by my side,
Be it dawn or noon or even tide.

Mum, how do you spend your time in heaven,
Do you still try calling me at eleven?

I LOOK BACK ON MEMORIES

I look back on memories I forgot I had,
At times I smile, but it hurts so bad.
I'd give anything to see your face
As none on earth can take your place.

I miss you more than words can say
The pain in my heart from that dreadful day.
That longest day, then night, then morn.
Clueless that, soon you'd be gone.

Clasping your hand so warm in mine
Who knew we were running out of time.
Now a photo I look at to see your smile,
Your number's saved on my speed dial

A video I watch to hear your voice,
This I do, for lack of choice.
I wonder how you're doing, Mum,
It's hard to focus, I feel so numb.

I pleaded with you not to leave,
For that would cause me so much grief.
But you would humbly say to me,
"What use am I to the family".

And I'd reply "More than you know,
You're our support, you help us grow".
Yet you had planned to have your way,
Depressed with lockdown and home stay.

So on angels wings you flew away,
No warning sign in the old month of May.
It's six whole months since you've been gone,
But the emptiness in me still lingers on.

If only I had a time machine,
I'd rewind to moments that had been.
I now recall memories I forgot I had,
They bring to life both you and dad.

ALL YOU'VE LEFT BEHIND

There's a lipstick on the dresser where you left it,
There's that old familiar perfume on the shelf,
Your cell phone on the pillow,
Your phone book lying fallow,
And the night light flickers dimly but its lit.

Your wardrobe has your clothes arranged so neatly,
Your footwear on the floor all in a line,
Crossword puzzles in a corner,
The room of your aroma,
So typical and easy to define.

Fancy stickers, coloured pens, glue and papers on your desk,
They don't seem to notice that you've gone.
The empty fridge, unfinished meds,
The clock that ticks above your bed,
Your mobile phone has had no ring for far too long.

Your Santa moulds and icing cones lie on the table,
The cherry stalks are waiting to be filled.
Cookie cutters trays and scones,
Silver balls and foil of gold,
All stacked in boxes that you neatly labeled

I've been scanning my phone viewing pictures,
Of last Christmas that the family spent with you.
The merriment song and laughter,
Your sweets that you had mastered,
Gift wrapping to which we have to say adieu.

And here we look around at empty spaces -
With memories of happy days gone by,
Your letters, cards and paintings,
The books you wrote are waiting;
Our heavy hearts won't let us say goodbye.

HAPPY BIRTHDAY MUM

At 12 am I dialed in,
But your phone just seemed to ring.
No answer from the other side,
And my heart began to sink.

So just in case you've changed your code,
Please share it with me Mum.
I long to hear your tender voice,
Need guidance from above.

Is there a party up in Heaven,
To celebrate today?
Did the angels bake a cake for you,
And sing to start your day?

Your date of birth was always special,
As we gathered round you here,
And phone calls were continuous,
From people far and near.

I miss those priceless moments,
That we shared throughout the years,
It's hard to think that on this day,
My eyes are filled with tears

I'm trying my best to smile for you,
I know that's what you'd want;
But every time I close my eyes,
The memories start to haunt

I wish you a Happy Birthday Mum,
Thank you for all you've done,
Keep smiling now from where you are,
With the Father and the Son.

MUM IN HEAVEN

For those who seek my mum in heaven,
She'll be easily identified –
Nimble, petite, God's masterpiece,
Gentle, one of a kind.

She'll be planting in heavens flower beds,
Flowers and ferns - the rarest kind,
And skillfully crafting birthday cards,
For each grandchild to remind.

Her floral gown you cannot miss,
She sings a lullaby,
Playing with the smallest angels,
A twinkle in her eye.

She's with her parents, and my dad,
And meets her long-lost friends,
No burden does she have to bear,
In that land love never ends.

And amidst her many activities,
Her thoughts still full of us,
She'll be watching from heaven's balcony,
To know just what's the buzz!

MY MUM A STAR

There's a star that twinkles bright at night,
That's stationed in the sky
And every time I look at it,
I needn't wonder why.

Though miles away it seems so near,
 That I try to reach up high
But all in vain I find it hard,
No matter how I try.

That special star is you I know,
Radiating pure joy and love
And looking down upon us all,
From miles and miles above.

This radiant glow with which you shine,
Is of a special kind;
It's filled with warmth and steadfast love,
So rare and hard to find.

But that is you and only you,
A wondrous beautiful soul
Too beautiful for this harsh mean world,
One with a heart of gold.

A few months ago you left us all,
For a brighter galaxy
Without a word without a sigh,
You flew so quietly

Although we know you're happy there,
We really miss you Ma
We miss your touch your gentle kiss,
Your phone calls every hour.

And so I look up at the sky,
Each night to have a peek
At that gleaming star that shines so bright,
And so I solace seek.

LIVE LIFE TO THE FULLEST

Cherish who you are,
And play by the rule
Don't be a critic,
Try not to be cruel.

Never look back
At what might have been
Let bygones be bygones,
On your past do not lean.

Give of yourself,
And all that you can
It's only with giving,
You'll feel like a man.

A confident soul
With no inhibition
Ready to conquer,
with no opposition.

Dance like no one's looking
Cry in the rain
So no one will notice,
Your anguish and pain.

Smile when you're angry,
Laugh when you're scared;
Always be humble,
Towards people you dread

Build highways that lead
To a better tomorrow
Reach for your dreams,
In troubles don't wallow.

Push negative thoughts
Right under the bridge,
With your head held high,
You'll get over the ridge.

Keep smiling with confidence
Greeting each brand-new day
Spread love and sunshine,
In your own unique way.

You have only one life
To treasure and care
So live it to the fullest,
Don't just stand and stare!

ABOUT THE AUTHOR

Lyncia Creado

The poet, Lyncia, is a devoted wife, mother of three and a woman of many talents. An interior designer by profession, she also sings, has acted in Theatre and is a culinary expert. She has directed many stage plays and skits for children in India, Dubai and Seychelles, where she taught drama in schools. Her love for poetry started young, reciting the works of Shakespeare at age 2, and winning numerous elocution competitions. During her free time, Lyncia writes stories, composes song lyrics and poems. She hails from a well-known East Indian family of the d'Almeidas and Correas of Mumbai, India.